From Trash to Treasures

Buttons and Beads

Daniel Nunn

Heinemann Library
Chicago, Illinois

www.heinemannraintree.com
Visit our website to find out
more information about
Heinemann-Raintree books.

To order:
☎ Phone 888-454-2279
▣ Visit www.heinemannraintree.com
to browse our catalog and order online.

© 2011 Heinemann Library
an imprint of Capstone Global Library, LLC
Chicago, Illinois

Edited by Rebecca Rissman, Daniel Nunn, and
Sian Smith
Designed by Joanna Hinton-Malivoire
Picture research by Tracy Cummins
Originated by Capstone Global Library Ltd
Printed in the United States of America in Stevens
Point, Wisconsin.

062011
006257RP

**Library of Congress Cataloging-in-Publication
Data**
Nunn, Daniel.
  Buttons and beads / Daniel Nunn.—1.
    pages cm.—(From Trash to Treasures)
  Includes bibliographical references and index.
  ISBN 978-1-4329-5152-8 (hc)—ISBN 978-1-4329-
5161-0 (pb) 1. Button craft—Juvenile literature. 2.
Beadwork—Juvenile literature. 3. Scrap materials—
Juvenile literature. I. Title.
  TT880.N86 2011
  745.58'4—dc22   2010049827

Acknowledgments
We would like to thank the following for permission
to reproduce photographs: Heinemann Raintree
pp. 4, 5, 6, 8, 9, 10, 11, 12, 13, 14, 15, 16, 17, 18, 19, 20,
21, 22, 23a, 23b (Karon Dubke); istockphoto pp. 7
(© Rob Hill), 23e (© Mostafa Hefni); Shutterstock
pp. 23c (© Jaren Jai Wicklund), 23d (© Denis and
Yulia Pogostins).

Cover photograph of flowers in homemade vases
reproduced with permission of Photolibrary (Radius
Images). Cover inset image of buttons and beads
and back cover images of a bracelet and flowers
reproduced with permission of Heinemann Raintree
(Karon Dubke).

Every effort has been made to contact copyright
holders of material reproduced in this book. Any
omissions will be rectified in subsequent printings if
notice is given to the publisher.

Disclaimer
All the Internet addresses (URLs) given in this book
were valid at the time of going to press. However,
due to the dynamic nature of the Internet, some
addresses may have changed, or sites may have
changed or ceased to exist since publication. While
the author and publisher regret any inconvenience
this may cause readers, no responsibility for any
such changes can be accepted by either the
author or the publisher.

Contents

Some words are shown in bold, **like this**. You can find them in the glossary on page 23.

What Are Buttons and Beads?

A bead is a small round object with a hole through the middle.

Beads are used to make necklaces or to **decorate** clothes.

A button is a small object that is used to **fasten** clothes.

Buttons and beads can be made from lots of different **materials**.

What Happens When You Throw Buttons and Beads Away?

Buttons and beads can look nice and be very useful.

But when you are finished with them, do you throw them away?

If so, then your buttons and beads will end up at a garbage dump.

They will be buried in the ground and may stay there for a very long time.

How Can I Reuse Old Buttons and Beads?

You can use old buttons and beads to make your own new things.

When you have finished with a button or a bead, put it somewhere safe.

Soon you will have lots of buttons
and beads waiting to be reused.

You are ready to turn your trash
into treasures!

What Can I Make with Buttons and Beads?

Buttons and beads can be turned into beautiful jewelry.

These beads have been made into a bracelet.

You can also use buttons and beads to make rings, necklaces, and other jewelry.

They can be whatever color you want!

This picture has been put together using old buttons.

Can you make your own button or bead art?

These flowers have been made with buttons, too!

They would make a perfect Mother's Day present.

What Can I Decorate with Buttons and Beads?

Buttons and beads make amazing decorations.

You can use them to make clothes look nicer.

You can also use them to **decorate** boxes.

Why not turn a boring old box into something you want to keep?

You can use buttons to **decorate** old flowerpots.

Try to find buttons that will match the color of the flowers you made earlier.

In fact, you can use buttons and beads to decorate almost anything!

Make Your Own Button and Bead Creatures

You can use buttons and beads to make some very strange creatures.

You will need buttons, beads, **pipe cleaners**, googly eyes, and craft glue.

First, use your **imagination** to decide what sort of creature you would like to make.

Then, start to thread the pipe cleaners through the buttons and beads.

Next, twist the **pipe cleaners** into different shapes to make your creature's body parts.

You could make arms, legs, wings, tails, horns, or shells.

Finally, use the craft glue to stick some eyes on your creature.

Now it is time to make your creature some friends. You could make a whole zoo!

Button Game

If you have any buttons left, you could play a game of tiddlywinks!

To play, shoot small buttons into a cup by pressing them with a large button.

Glossary

 **decorate** add something fancy to something plain to make it look nicer

 **fasten** connect something or tie something together

 **imagination** thinking up ideas or seeing pictures of things in your head

 **material** what something is made of

 **pipe cleaner** piece of bendable wire covered in fluffy material

Find Out More

Ask an adult to help you make fun things with buttons and beads using the Websites below.

Button pictures: **www.bhg.com/crafts/kids/rainy-day/kids-crafts-buttons/?page=4**

Flowers: **http://pbskids.org/zoom/activities/do/buttonflowers.html**

Jewelry: **http://familyfun.go.com/crafts/bedazzling-beaded-jewelry-845038/**

You can find other ideas at: **http://crafts.kaboose.com/wear/bead-crafts.html**

Index